Strong and Tender

A guide for the father whose baby has died

By
Pat Schwiebert, RN
Director, Perinatal Loss, Grief Watch

Illustrations by
Jean Grover

Acknowledgements

What can I say but thank you to the men I have known over the past 20 years who have been willing to teach me what it's like to be a bereaved father by sharing their stories. They have been willing to lay their hearts open, and to remember that instant in which their lives were changed by a wished-for child – one for whom they were ready to be strong and one who would expect them to be tender, too. I especially thank Jon Weaver, Steve Daggett, Joe Lowe, Craig Bryant, Russ Rottiers, Jeff Johnson, and Cliff Hewlett for their contributions to this booklet.

Strong as the foundation of an old oak tree, he protects and comforts his own.

Table of Contents

I've always like

a fast-paced work schedule

a fleeting smile

strong sure feet

glistening race horses

quick service.

I just haven't learned to appreciate

how quickly you went through my life.

Introduction

Fatherhood has taken an unexpected turn in your life. Your baby has died, your partner needs you in a whole new way, and there are many decisions to make. You are in a state of shock and disbelief – the beginning of a grief process that will be with you and your family for a long time. And you are expected to be strong.

You are not just a man who happened to be married to a pregnant woman. You played an important role in this pregnancy. The growth and expansion of your family was happening to both you and your partner at the same time and, though the pregnancy was impacting the two of you on different levels, it was a mutual experience. Likewise, the death of your little one has happened to you both, at a profound level.

Unfortunately, there will be a tendency for medical professionals and society in general to see you in a supporting role to the grieving mother of your child, rather than to acknowledge you as a bereaved parent in your own right. Though you might actually be more comfortable in this supporting role and seek refuge in it, it is a position that can actually negate your significant role as a bereaved father. Because you also are very tender.

Your grief because of the death of your baby will not remain an isolated experience. You will feel its impact in all aspects of your life; marriage, your work, your close friendships – all will be affected. At times you may want to run from the reality of grief. But you cannot hide. Grief will seek you out.

This book is intended to help you, the bereaved father, to understand in general terms the kind of work which grief requires, and then to find your own unique and personal ways of expressing your sorrow – ways that take into account your own particular upbringing and that provide you with the comfort which works for you. Also, besides offering you some important self-help tools, the book is designed to provide you with some ways to offer emotional and spiritual support for your family during this difficult time.

Most of all, we hope this book will affirm your role to be both Strong and Tender.

Everyday courage has few witnesses.
But yours is no less noble
because no drum beats before you,
and no crowds shout your name.

Robert Louis Stevenson

About Being a Man in Our Culture

People grieve in very different ways – even two parents who grieve the death of the same baby. How people grieve is affected by age, previous life experiences, personality, culture, gender, and by whatever else may be happening in their lives at the time of the loss. Because of these differing factors, you may find yourself relating more to some parts of this book than to other parts.

As a father, your experience of grief is probably going to differ from that of your partner, not only because you are not the one who has been carrying the baby inside of your body, but simply because you and your partner are two different people with different backgrounds and different ways of acting and reacting. Cultural conditioning, spoken and unspoken assumptions, and other influences will communicate to you some very clear messages about how others think you are to behave. It is important to find the way of grief that works for you, and not be dependent on other's expectations.

Women tend to express grief more openly than do men, but that does not necessarily mean that women feel grief more deeply than do men. Because of this difference, however, the grieving mother of a child who has died typically gets more of the attention, while the father is kept from getting the support and help he needs to adequately grieve the death of their baby. And yet at the same time, fathers often have been chided or criticized if they did not openly express grief in the same way, or to the same degree as their partner.

As a man you are typically expected to:
be strong
appear "in control"
appear confident
show more interest in thinking than in feeling
endure pain
be brave
get mad
be assertive
be the protector
be the provider
take charge

4

As a man you are typically expected *not* to:
> cry in front of others
> appear weak
> seem insecure
> be afraid
> be dependent
> ask for help
> get depressed
> lose control

These gender related and culturally imposed characteristics may serve you well in day-to-day living, but as a grieving father these same attributes may make the task of successful grieving difficult, if not impossible.

Women generally have fewer conflicts between their traditional upbringing and the requirements of mourning, such as confiding in others, showing emotion, and the accepting of temporary regression.

Some of the culturally impossible factors that may contribute to your unconscious resistance to grief and your not permitting grief to flow through you are listed below:

> not being able to openly express feelings of pain or loss
> not being able to accept help from others
> not allowing yourself to slow down
> not being able to seek emotional support

Grief work requires a willingness to do almost the opposite of what you may want to do to solve this problem. Grief work requires that you:

> Talk about your feelings rather than suppress them.
> Acknowledge your sense of powerlessness.

Your automatic response to grief
will most likely be to overcome grief
rather than to experience it.

Instinctively Alone

Where does a man go to grieve his woundedness,

especially when society sees it as weakness,

to be self pity?

I desperately need validation,

so I can be with my pain,

so I can embrace the truth of my life.

I can't believe how well I've been trained to

stoically stash the losses in my life.

I feel like a wounded animal, instinctively

returning to the graveyard of my ancestors to die.

Hush!

Go to your room.

As a boy I was ordered to travel alone.

Now suffer the agony of manhood,

as I enter the garden of stone.

R.M. Hastie

"What's a Father to do?"
by John Weaver

It starts when you're a kid, with the unmistakable message: "Big boys don't cry." In Little League and Pop Warner they told you to "walk it off." Today, when men are sick, they go to the office, not to the doctor. Be strong. Play hard. When our daughter Kathleen Marie, or Kate as we refer to her, was stillborn four days before her due date, the same subtleties were there.

Naturally, pregnancy focuses on the mother and child more than on the father, in much the same way as the typical wedding focuses on the bride more than on the groom. It's a quaint custom which nearly every bridegroom faces, as does almost every father-to-be. The father/groom becomes an accessory, an ancillary part of the process.

The marginalization of the expectant father begins early in the pregnancy, and may be accompanied by crude comments when the pregnancy is announced, such as "Well, your job is done!" Make no mistake about it. You are being moved aside. Others have defined your role, and you are viewed as a supporting actor, not a principal. The problem with this view is that when you experience a loss, you are still on the outside. The baby's death is viewed as less of a loss for you than for the child's mother.

"How's your wife doing?" was the question. "I know you'll take good care of her." It became clear that I was a sideline observer to the loss of our daughter. Be strong. She needs you. The message was unmistakable. Friends expected her to grieve, but they didn't have the same expectation of me. My job was only to be there for her, so she could grieve.

To be honest, though, I accept this cultural expectation at certain levels, even though I prefer to deny it.

In this new and sensitive age in which we live, both men and women can cook, clean, do laundry and take parental leave

8

(note: no longer "maternity" leave, but "parental" leave). Still, most of us have grown up with well-defined and differentiated gender expectations. No matter what we say, surveys still show that women cook and clean more often than do men. When I walk around the neighborhood on a summer Saturday, I see a lot more men than women washing cars and mowing lawns. Women plant flowers and men mow lawns. It's the same cultural role-playing that leads me to insist that I will be the one up on the ladder stringing Christmas lights on the roof. "No, really, it's not a gender thing – but I'll get it." Yeah, right. And for most men, actually taking twelve weeks of unpaid parental leave is a career decision. "Oh sure, you can, but you know…"

"It's not a gender thing," I insist. So why does it bug me that my wife brings home a bigger paycheck than I do? It's because in an age of equality, I was brought up to know that I'm supposed to be the breadwinner, the provider, the hunter. More often than not, we men are told we shouldn't feel this way. Maybe it's not "correct," maybe we know better, but there it is. All those lessons we grew up with are there when we need them least.

All those messages are about what makes a man. When Dad was getting ready to leave on a business trip, he said, "You be the man of the house while I'm gone." (read: take care of the women and small children.) "You look out for your sister." I can recite these expectations by heart. Intellectually, I can refute every one of them. But here they come again – baggage from my past that I can't seem to discard.

So at what point is a man entitled to mourn? We may say it's ok for a man to feel pain, to cry. But most of us still hear those voices about what is expected of a man – all of those messages we heard growing up. Physically and emotionally, men are supposed to be strong and this means not expressing strong emotions. We talk confidently about breaking down stereotypes, but the game we play is very different.

How does a "man" grieve for his little girl, especially when she

9

never drew a breath, never cried. How does a dad grieve for his stillborn daughter when he never changed a diaper or warmed a bottle? How does he feel when it seems like others don't even think of him as a father at all, since he never got to play the father role? After all, the mother is the one who carried the baby, not you, Dad. The mother is the one who felt every movement, not you, Dad. The mother is the one who was pregnant, not you, Dad. Even friends assume that the "bond" is only between the mother and child, at least until the child is born.

That is why I had waited so eagerly for Kate. With every kick and move, I anticipated the day when I would finally get to meet her face to face. But that day never came. I never got to do anything with her. That was the nature of my loss. Long awaited, eagerly anticipated, she was gone before we met. A near miss. Yes, I was once-removed, waiting my turn. But my turn and my daughter never came.

True, I didn't have an intimate connection with her yet. But that doesn't mean it hurt any less; that is precisely why and how it hurts.

Grief is lonely. And grief because of a pregnancy loss is lonelier still. It is the most silent of losses for men and women, but especially men.

Men typically don't share with each other the emotional intimacy that women share. Forgive the sweeping generalization, but women tend to do better at articulating their feelings, and they tend to do so more freely than men.

Bereaved fathers typically have their work cut out for them right off the bat. After Kate was born, my wife needed to be taken care of, physically and emotionally. Physically, she was healing from labor and delivery. Emotionally we were both wrecks, but in different ways. And while we didn't have our baby, the attendant post-partum depression was there. No baby, just blues.

In addition to trying to be there for my wife, I had a memorial service to plan. I threw myself into the task, knowing that this was the only gift I would ever be able to give my daughter. It was also something in my life which I could grab hold of and control, a very attractive prospect when everything else seemed so out of control or irrelevant.

I took two weeks off from work. Because ours was a late April loss, I wanted to be with my wife through Mother's Day. When I did return to work, I felt awkward and strange. Most people were very kind. But others avoided me, not knowing what to say – not quite realizing that there was nothing to say, and that that's okay. Some went to ridiculous lengths to deny the obvious. Once I arrived at the office puffy-eyed after a morning spent thinking about Kate only to have one person comment, "Yeah, must be some kind of pollen out today."

In addition to feeling like I had failed, I felt like damaged goods. A whole room full of people would suddenly fall silent when I walked in, as if people were waiting for me to lose my composure, as if they were afraid to speak to me for fear that they might cause me to break down emotionally.

And that's not how men are supposed to be. We're supposed to be strong. Adaptive. Roll with the punches. Deal with it.

I had a problem even caring about my work. My job as a fundraiser for the Athletic Department at Oregon State University, and college sports in general, just didn't seem to matter anymore.

Life was slower. I drove more slowly and wondered what the rush was about. What did it matter? Life goes on, the now-ironic saying goes. It would just have to go on without us for a while.

We would just have each other, sometimes.

We knew immediately that the loss of Kate could either bring us closer together or tear us apart. That's how it is with any

11

experience that impels growth. We knew each of us would grow. The question was, would we grow together or would we grow apart?

I had looked upon Kate as an entity distinct from her mother. My wife viewed Kate more as a part of herself. Where she had lost a part of herself, I had lost someone with whom I had never been joined. Kate's death meant to my wife that she could no longer love and care for that part of herself. But I had never had the opportunity to love and care for our daughter at all.

Without the same connection to Kate that my wife enjoyed, I approached grief from a more spiritual perspective, spending time in Kate's room and finding reasons to return to our house immediately after the loss, even though we were staying with my wife's parents. I needed somehow to gain a sense of my daughter's presence. I never felt the need to ask why she died. If I asked why she died, I might as well ask why she lived. Ultimate questions aren't that easy to answer.

My wife didn't ask what went wrong. She asked, " What did I do to cause this?" Had she been working too hard, not taking care of herself? She remembered the time she had said, in the midst of lay-offs at work, "What a lousy time to be pregnant!" and she wondered if she was being punished for not being more grateful for the gift that was growing inside of her. Seeking answers, she turned her questions upon herself.

The differences between the two of us were not limited to how we looked at Kate. Timing was an issue. My wife had assumed that she and I would move through our grief at about the same pace. The reality was quite the opposite, and more intriguing, really. We developed an intuitive pattern. I wouldn't call it an "emotional roller coaster;" teeter-totter is a better metaphor. When I was down and feeling vulnerable, she would be up and feeling strong; and when she was down and feeling vulnerable, I would be up and feeling strong. We came to sense when it was time to change, when the other had been strong long enough and was about to crash, and when it was the other person's turn to be tough.

I had read that it was common for men to have a delayed grief reaction, to feel the loss more intensely a year or more later. It happened to me just six months after we lost Kate.

Grief can be a lot like Christmas, in that it simply amplifies whatever is already going on in family relationships – a Brady Family Christmas or Yuletide in Dysfunction Junction.

As Christmas approached that year, I had a major set back. I had felt furious at my sister for not coming to the hospital soon enough, at my brother for staying in Seattle when his in-laws had offered to fly him down. Never mind that he and his wife had given birth to a daughter two weeks before we lost Kate. My resentment had simmered for six months, and when the annual "because-we're-such-a-close-family-we-must-all-do-the-holidays-thing" talk began, it was too much.

Two weeks after I writ these words it will have been two years since we lost Kate. My partner and I will both take time off to spend time with each other and with our 10-month-old child, Grace Kathleen. We'll go away for a couple of days, and later do some work in our garden. We have developed ways of building ritual into our lives to help us remember Kate. A new dogwood tree in our front yard is in full pink bloom every April on her birthday. At Christmas, her stocking holds its rightful place, and an angel tops our tree. A pink candle lights our mantle.

I fought hard to remember her, to remember her face. Though I vowed that I would not forget, I was terrified that I would forget. I was crushed the first time I realized that I had gone through an entire day without thinking about her. But as Kate's second birthday approaches, though the memories soften, they do not fade. Periodically a memory or association will grab me and shake me, stopping me in my tracks, and I am thankful that I am still susceptible to that.

13

I realize that we are doing what I thought we could never do. Gently we are getting along, going on. Being strong in a tender way. Stronger in a way than a Pop Warner coach could never have imagine d a man could be.

The difference between a man's and a woman's feelings about their baby's death is this: A woman tends to feel that something has been take from her. A man tends to feel that something was never given to him.

Steve Richter

While at the Hospital

Following are some ways you can help manage the time in the hospital before, during and after delivery.

Arrange to be together with your partner whenever the doctor comes to share information about your baby.

Don't try to protect your partner by discouraging her from seeing your baby who has died or is dying in the mistaken belief that separation from the child will lessen her pain.

Make decisions together as much as possible.

Don't agree to funeral arrangements that would exclude your partner, such as holding a memorial service before she is discharged from the hospital.

There will be times when you will need to be strong and in control even though your controlled behavior may cause others to think that you don't care. Be sure that you share your true feelings with your partner – and that you also give yourself time to let down(?). Let her see your tender side, too.

Invite those who are close to you to come to the hospital to see and hold your baby. As you expand the circle of friends who get to share this experience, you will enable more of them to help you down the road because they will have a clearer sense of what your grief is all about.

Take pictures of your baby, and ask someone else to take pictures of you and your partner holding the baby.

Stay overnight in the hospital with your partner if you can.

Don't send someone to your house to empty the nursery and put the baby things away, even if they offer to do this in a sincere effort to be helpful. That task needs to wait for you and your partner to take care of in your own time. If the presence of an empty crib and unused baby things seems like too painful a reminder of your loss, close the door to the child's room. There is no set time frame that determines when it is best to put the baby items away or pass them on to someone else. Many parents find that the baby's room is a place where they will go to do their grieving time in the days to come.

Your partner's release from the hospital may well be a sensitive and difficult time for both of you; on the one hand, because of the painful reminder that you are leaving without a child in your arms, and on the other hand, because it's your first venture into the public as bereaved parents. Having nothing but a potted plant in your arms may add to your already profound sense of failure. And there is no foolproof way to make your exit unnoticed. The fear of someone inquiring about the baby is normal. Not making eye contact usually works at other times in your life when you don't want to strike up a conversation with someone. It should work now also.

If your baby is born alive

If your baby has survived labor and delivery, yet is barely clinging to life with little hope for survival, you will have special challenges to face beyond those confronted by the parents of a stillborn child. And if your partner's health is also compromised, you may find yourself needing to divide your time between the Neonatal Intensive Care Unit and the Maternity Unit, wanting to be in both places at the same time. The scenario will be worse yet if the baby is in one hospital and the mother in another.

Try to remember as much of the experience with your child as you can, so that later you can share it with your partner. Fathers who have this experience will most likely bond with the baby more, and initially even grieve the loss more, than will the mother, who is preoccupied with her own health. For her, the onset of grief may be somewhat delayed, but it will come eventually. She may experience jealousy because you were able to spend time with the baby while she could not. Taking pictures and sharing all your experiences and feelings will help her to be more a part of the baby's life.

16

If Your Baby Died Early in the Pregnancy

Early pregnancy loss, commonly known as miscarriage, is one of the best-kept secrets in our society. At least 20 percent of all babies die spontaneously in utero during the early weeks of pregnancy. Yet, many people are not aware of anyone who has had an early pregnancy loss because it occurs before there are obvious signs of pregnancy, and/or because the parents have chosen not to reveal their loss.

Early pregnancy loss brings with it some unique difficulties because early pregnancy itself is often a confusing time marked by feelings of ambivalence. On the one hand, the parents want this baby, but on the other hand, there are doubts. Are we ready to take on this responsibility? Are we ready to give up the freedom we enjoy? Can we handle the financial burden of this new addition to our family?

Such anxieties, common to most expectant parents, tend to diminish later on in the pregnancy. But if your baby dies now in the midst of this confusion and ambivalence, the confusion and ambivalence are compounded. You may feel a sense of relief that the burden of responsibility has been lifted. But at the same time, you may experience guilt for not totally accepting your anticipated new role. You may even have an irrational belief that your ambivalence was what caused the baby to die.

During early pregnancy, it is quite normal for a father to feel less of an attachment to the baby than the mother does. Some reasons for this are that it is still to early to feel the baby move, it isn't your body that is changing, and your partner's body hasn't changed enough outwardly to draw attention to the pregnancy.

Still, for some men, the excitement of expecting a new little person in their family matches or even exceeds that of their partner. They may see fatherhood as the most important role in their life. Most men don't realize the importance of being a father until after the baby is born, but some men anticipate fatherhood, dream about parenting and are actively preparing themselves emotionally and spiritually for what is to come.

Some women who experience an early pregnancy loss may be noticeably down for only a few weeks, and though they may continue to be sad after that, the grief does not consume them. For other women, however, the loss of this pregnancy will be every bit as painful as will be the loss experienced by a mother whose baby died at the end of pregnancy.

Your emotions as a bereaved father may range from indifference to a sense of enormous loss in your life. If you and your partner have been trying to conceive for a long time or have experienced yet another loss, you will probably feel a strong sense of disappointment (maybe even rage) at having your future as a parent taken away from you. You may feel resentment at how easy it seems to be for other people to achieve parenthood. Added to these feelings may be a sense of humiliation at the supposed failure of your masculinity, and your sadness at watching your partner grieve.

It was so small, this little piece of life just beginning to form, that you had attached your future to. Until it happens to us, we cannot fully appreciate how an early pregnancy loss can consume such a huge amount of our energy as it sucks the wind out of our sails and thoroughly demoralizes us. It is humbling to admit how we take our fertility for granted, until something like this reminds us of our vulnerability.

Future pregnancies may feel tentative and your enthusiasm or desire to become attached to this new little person may be somewhat guarded until you are well into the pregnancy. Because of men's seeming ability to adapt easier to life's little setbacks, you may tend to take on the role of cheerleader. For the most part, your chances of achieving your goal of having a baby are statistically very good. Some men have shared that they just took on the attitude that they'll just keep trying until they are successful, remembering that sometimes people have to work harder than others do to get what they want. Fairness has nothing to do with it.

18

Dear Baby Boy,

It seems like a long time since last year when we first learned you had entered our lives. I remember being very sure that you would be OK and join us in our physical world. I was so excited when I saw your heart beating in the ultrasound picture. Since I don't get to experience physical pregnancy, that moment really made me realize that you were there, growing, and on your way into our lives.

I was so disappointed when we later learned that you had died. We could see on the second ultrasound that you had grown a lot, but your heart was not beating.

I felt cheated out of getting to know you, and cheated that Molly wouldn't get to know you either. We tell her about you sometimes.

Our family of three is what I'm getting used to, but I always think about what it would have been like had you been able to join us. Thank you for showing me (again) just how precious life is, and how blessed we are to be a family of three.

Love,

Daddy

I Promise

I promise to help us laugh again.

I promise to honor the different ways we grieve our baby's death.

I promise to honor your thoughts and feelings.

I promise to cherish you with all my heart.

I promise to tell you my truth in a loving way.

I promise to treat you as an equal.

I promise to trust your journey.

I promise never to forget our baby.

I needed to be alone because
I was so busy taking care of others' feelings,
I couldn't find my own.
But then I was afraid of finding
my own feelings and becoming so immersed
in them that I would never emerge.

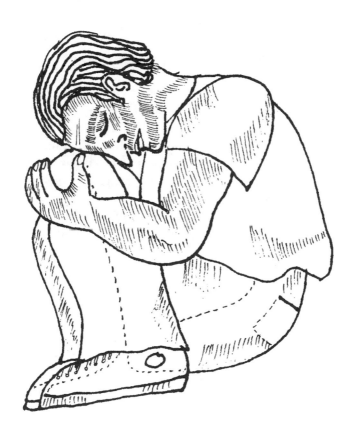

What if You Don't Experience a Profound Sense of Loss?

You may be one of those persons who experiences a loss as just a normal part of life. You may be better able than most to roll with the punches. It's not that you aren't feeling bad it turned out this way, and that there's no new baby to bring home. It's just that this is the way you've always dealt with life's disappointments. You pick yourself up, you shake yourself off and you get on with your life.

Does this mean that you are a jerk, an insensitive guy whom no woman deserves? Probably not. However, if you are the husband of a woman who is deeply grieving, she may be less than accepting of your more philosophical approach to life right now. She may indeed feel like scratching your eyes out.

So what are you to do?

First, you will need to be patient with her. Take care not to put her down in subtle ways, because she is grieving in the way that is more natural to her. It is important for you to be present with her in ways that acknowledge her special grief. Caring for a grieving partner is a lot like dancing. It will never work if one of you insists on doing a slow waltz and the other is doing a fast two-step. Follow her lead. If she is quiet and pensive, don't try to snap her out of it by joking around or by being loud. Just being in the room with her will at least let her know you care and aren't put off by her behavior. Continue being present wither even though it takes much longer than you want it to.

After a while, you may want to get involved in some projects around the house. However, don't become so engrossed in your own activities that she feels abandoned. Check in with her regularly. The more attentive you can be, the better. Don't just assume that what you are doing is right for her, however. Ask her what will be most helpful to her. She may know, but then again, she may not know how to answer. Be patient and understanding of her lack of certainty. Nothing seems certain anymore.

When you are at a loss to understand your partner's feelings – feelings that are very different from your own – resist the temptation to resort to sarcasm as a way of communicating your annoyance. A good motto for times like this is, "Never give up the opportunity to keep your mouth shut." Remind yourself that whatever momentary relief you may get from making a dig at your partner is probably not worth the potential harm to your relationship.

How long will this go on? You can assume it will last longer than you want it to… much longer. You may want to refer to the chapter on "How Long will Grief be Your Companion."

Life does not accommodate you,
it shatters you. It is meant to
and couldn't do better. Every seed
destroys its container or else
there would be no growth, no fruition

Florida Scott Maxwell

I Laugh and Cry with the Same Eyes

I laugh and cry with the same eyes.
Love and hate with the same heart.
I feel my rage and my gentleness,
my sanity and suicide.

When I hide my anger, my joy doesn't seem real.
If I only laugh, I leave no place for your pain.
When I hide my fear, my strength is a fraud.
If I only shout, I leave no place for your tenderness.

I want to be all of myself
  so you can be all of yourself,
    and together we can be whole.

James Kavanaugh

There is a bridge between our worlds – this life and the other. It is the same bridge that is within us as body and soul, between conscious thought and our dreams. As more of our loved ones cross this bridge, we make more visits until we are so familiar with this bridge, we can cross it in the dark and even in our sleep.

I Let You Inside

I let you inside.
I wasn't going to
   it just happened.
I thought I'd wait
   till I got to know you
      till after you were born,
         but something happened
            without my realizing.
And now you are dead
   and I am mad that I let you inside.
Because if I hadn't let you in
I wouldn't hurt.
And God knows, I don't like to feel pain.

So I'll shut you out
   so I can survive
      at least till I can figure out
         how to do it right.

For if I grieve now,
surely I will die, too.

You leave us closer than before –
forever changed and connected
with new names you gave us –
Father, Uncle, Grandfather.

Things You can do for Your Baby

One of the things many bereaved fathers miss is the opportunity to do something for their baby. Death has taken away the occasion for doing and giving, but the need to do and to give is still there. Your partner brought forth life from her womb (with your help), and now you may want to release some creative energy, too. Here are some suggestions of things you can do in the face of a loss, based upon what other fathers have done for or on behalf of their babies.

If you are planning a burial, make the baby's casket yourself, or in the event of cremation, build an urn for the baby's ashes.

Buy the clothing in which the baby will be buried or cremated.

Plan the memorial service.

Write a poem or a letter to be used at the memorial service.

Build a memory chest in which to store away your precious memories of your child.

Plant a rose bush or tree in memory of your baby.

Write a song for your baby.

Purchase a child's book and donate it to your local library as a memorial to your child.

Donate altar flowers to your church or synagogue in your child's memory.

Volunteer with a local organization working with children or some other cause to which you feel drawn.

I'll never buy
  her prom dress
 or the gown she'd choose
    for her wedding day,
but I will buy the only dress
  she'll ever wear.

Expressing Intimacy During Bereavement

Lovemaking, an activity that used to bring you joy, comfort and a sense of closeness, may now be a wedge between you and your partner during the time of your bereavement. While you may have a strong desire for sexual intercourse, your partner may show a complete lack of interest.

This difference is not uncommon. Some women who are experiencing perinatal grief have no desire for sexual intercourse. They may not even be capable of sexual arousal because the experience of loss is so fresh in their mind. They may believe they don't deserve to feel good, or that it is inappropriate for them to experience pleasure, when their baby is dead. Still others are afraid of another pregnancy and with it the prospect of facing yet another death; hence anything that remotely reminds them of pregnancy, or involves a risk of pregnancy is out of the question.

Never assume that what you want is what your partner wants. Her real need may be for closeness in the form of touching and gentle caressing that does not lead to intercourse. Yet, she may be afraid of initiating demonstrations of affection if she has reason to believe that you will interpret such affection as a prelude to sexual intercourse.

Advice from many fathers who have moved through the experience of bereavement is, "No matter how much you desire sexual intercourse with your partner, don't push for it." Be understanding and patient. You may have to settle for masturbation as your sexual outlet for the time being. Give your partner the affection she needs without the pressure to go further, and wait until she indicates that she is ready.

Some people get intimacy and sexual intercourse confused. Intimacy between partners may or may not include sexual intercourse. Intimacy is a deep connection with another person that says, "I care. I share myself with you. I am willing to be vulnerable with you and to put aside any fears or suspicions as I enter into this relationship with you. I am willing to trust you with who I am right now.

31

I will not violate or take advantage of you. I want to just be with you – with no hidden agendas or strings attached. I care enough to take the risk of being rejected."

The following are some simple ways to express and nurture intimacy:

> Take a walk together holding hands.
>
> Make eye contact that says I love you.
>
> Smile at your partner.
>
> Touch your partner lovingly,
> or offer a back rub or massage.
>
> Caress your partner's hair.
>
> Sit close to your partner with your arm
> around her as you watch TV together.

The object is not to see through one another,
but to see one another through.

Taking Care of Yourself

Being the "pillar of strength" that you are expected to be has its perils. If your role as protector supersedes your role as bereaved parent, you may suppress the feelings of grief you have by pushing them deep down inside you in order to take care of your family. You may even have fooled yourself into thinking that how you are acting on the outside is what you're feeling on the inside.

Grief can be very subtle. You may think you're handling things just fine after the initial shock of your baby's death has worn off. You aren't crying. You are able to function normally. You're sleeping pretty well. Compared to your partner, you seem to be pretty much on top of things. But grief is still there.

It's grief that makes you angry when you drive past a park where little kids are playing soccer. It's grief that takes the enthusiasm out of the job you used to like. It's grief that causes you to resent your friends who have kids.

This grief is normal and, thank goodness, usually temporary. By taking care of yourself, the throes of grief will be manageable.

Here are some ways to take care of yourself:

> Exercise, even if you don't feel like it. It won't take the grief away, but it will help reduce the pent-up stress caused by grief.

> Eat a balanced diet.

> Find a friend who will listen to your grief, or who is willing to just be with you in silence.

> Find constructive ways to vent your anger.

> Learn to recognize the symptoms and feelings that accompany grief so you can know when you're acting out of your grief.

Give yourself permission to play.

Give yourself permission to cry.

Do less rather than more.

Be careful not to over-indulge in your use of drugs or alcohol or in working overtime in a misguided attempt to keep from feeling the pain of your loss.

Tell your partner what you need from her.

Women cry.

Men become angry.

Women seek relationships and support.

Men seek to provide support and turn to action.

Taking Care of Your Partner

Even though we stress that your main role is that of a bereaved father, your concern for your partner's well-being is extremely important. Physically, she will be recovering from the birth, her hormones will be somewhat out of whack, and her body will most likely want to produce breast milk, adding a further reminder of her loss. If that's not bad enough, her regular clothes probably won't fit and she'll need to continue to wear maternity clothes. Each reminder will tend to increase her sense of failure and loss.

Below is a list of things you can do that may help your partner:

Buy her some new clothes, so she won't have to wear her maternity clothes.

Be a good listener. Encourage her to share her feelings with you.

Don't act annoyed if she needs to repeat the same things over and over again.

Write notes to her.

Call her when you are away.

Give her permission to grieve in her own way.

Be patient with her.

Find new ways to share intimacy.

Attend support group meetings with her, or encourage her to go to support groups and ask her to tell you about the experience.

Don't try to fix her. You can't.

Be mindful of times that will be most difficult, e.g. her first postpartum visit to the doctor, your baby's due date, Christmas, Mother's Day, Father's Day, family gatherings, baby showers, etc.

Be cautious about suggesting too soon that you try to have another baby.

Don't criticize her if she's grieving in a manner that you don't think is normal.

Avoid the impulse to minimize the loss, or to pretend it isn't a big deal.

She may feel she let you down in a very big way by denying you the privilege of having this baby that you both wanted. Remind her that you love her.

For me it was a coming event

For her it was an already existing relationship

Taking Care of Your Marriage/Relationship

A grieving partner is a partner in need, and meeting your partner's needs may take an exceptional amount of time, energy, patience and understanding. And because you too are a grieving partner, your own ability to care for someone else at this time may be somewhat limited.

Statistics suggest that a marriage is extremely vulnerable when the partners are grieving the death of a child. The likelihood of divorce is higher among bereaved couples than among couples in general. But keep in mind that the marriage success statistics for the general population are not all that impressive either.

Your risk is increased if the two of you are young and have never had to deal with a crisis of this magnitude together. Without any experience to draw upon, you have now way of knowing how either of you are likely to deal with the enormity of the stress involved. Nor can you know ahead of time that grief may be so physically and emotionally consuming that you simply will have too little energy to care for anyone other than yourself. It takes energy to care enough to work things out.

Don't assume, however, that a death sentence has been pronounced on your relationship and that there is no hope. There are things you can do. Your relationship can, in fact, be enhanced in spite of, and because of this terrible tragedy.

You may think that if you don't reveal your own disappointment or don't bring up the subject of your baby's death, you will somehow help diminish your partner's pain by helping her to forget. Believe us when we say there is no way you can diminish your partner's pain.

Here are some suggestions:

> Tell her what you need.
> Don't assume that she's a mind reader.
>
> Keep a sense of humor. But remember that timing is

everything.

Expect that your grief and her grief will probably not be alike, and that though you might start out feeling very connected to each other, within a short time your grief may look very different.

Keep on courting her. Keep the romance in your relationship.

Not right away, but at some point, talk about the pressure that this experience is adding to your sex life.

You may think you feel more concerned about her feelings that she does about yours. Expect that you won't be able entirely to meet each other's emotional, physical, or psychological needs. Don't set your expectations too high right now. Give each other some slack.

Keep an open mind about seeking counseling. Be willing to do whatever you need to do to save your marriage. You have lost your baby. Don't risk losing your marriage also.

In the months following the death of your child, you may be very vulnerable to an extra-marital relationship, not because you don't love your wife, but because you may be wanting comfort, and the chance to be with someone who is not constantly reminding you of your loss. A brief affair with another person may seem very appealing as an antidote for grief, because grief is not pretty. In fact, grief can be down right aggravating if you have to come home to it every night. This is a reality, and somehow you will need to find a way to allow your wife to grieve and not force her to stuff her grief in order to save your marriage. These words may seem harsh, and you may rather not hear them or believe it could happen to you; but it can.

Either you're pulling together or you're pulling apart. There really is no in-between.

Kobi Yamada

38

Taking Care of Your Other Children

One of the strongest evidences of the resiliency of children is that they can survive in a family of bereaved parents after a sibling has died. Your other children will be both a help and a hindrance to you in your time of bereavement.

Young children in particular need constant attention, and for a grieving parent who is emotionally preoccupied (a typical grief reaction), the ongoing neediness of your other children can also give you a chance to be distracted from your grief. This distraction can be a good thing if the attention you give to your other children allows you to get out of yourself for short periods of time. This distraction can have a negative effect, however, if it encourages you to put off your grief work.

Parents who have one surviving twin find this to be particularly true because they need to devote their immediate attention to the surviving twin and so are less free to submerge themselves in the grief process. The postponed grief will eventually surface and have to be dealt with. But for some people, grief will be more confusing and problematic at the later time.

Here are some suggestions to help you in your role as protector, nurturer and teacher to your surviving children:

> Include your other children in the hospital experience, especially if you have involved them in the pregnancy. If possible, let them see and hold the baby.

> Be honest with your children. Let them know how you feel. Don't be afraid to let them see you cry. That's one way you can help break down cultural stereotypes. Above all, don't try to hide your feelings from your children in the mistaken notion that secrecy will somehow protect them.

> Tell them the truth about the baby's death. Even young

children who don't have well developed verbal skills know more than you may think. A year after her little sister died, one three-year-old child, who was being taken to a doctor's appointment, asked, "Is this the doctor who keeps the babies?" even though she had never been told anything about the baby sibling who never came home from the hospital.

Read them storybooks that can help them understand death.

Be careful not to use euphemisms for death, such as "asleep" or "went away," which can scare or confuse children.

Listen to your children. Encourage them to talk about their feelings. If you don't know the answer to one of their questions, tell them so. If you gave them an answer that later you think might have been incorrect, you can always go back and talk about it.

Encourage children to use play as a way of acting out their thoughts and feelings.

Don't read a book about how children grieve and assume that's how your child will behave. Children, like adults, will each grieve in their own way, according to their own particular style.

Your Grief May Differ

She may want to talk.
    You may not.

You may find comfort in making love.
    She may not.

She may want you to visit the cemetery with her often.
    You may prefer to go alone.

You may want to move on with your life.
    She may not.

She may want to have another baby soon.
    You may not.

She may have fantasies and dreams of your baby.
    You may not.

She may want to leave the door to the nursery open.
    You may not.

She may want to look for deeper answers.
    You may want to accept the reality and quickly move on.

She may find comfort being at her mother's house.
    You may prefer being in your own space.

She may experience more headaches, sleep disturbances,
anxiety and depression, and reproductive, urinary and
gastrointestinal problems.
    You may be more inclined to experience musculoskeletal
    problems such as backaches, and problems arising from
    aggressive behavior, e.g. car accidents, abuse of alcohol
    and verbal arguments.

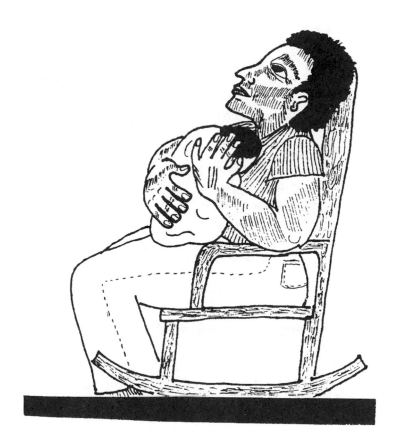

As a man I thought I was supposed to be in control – to be able to make things happen or to prevent things from happening. Not to be in control felt emasculating. If I am impotent to change things, am I still a man?

Katie and Alicia

Identical twins

26 weeks
3 months early
Not expected to live
But the did
Alicia for 10 ½ months
Katie is with us still

For that time
Not so long ago
Death was always with us
Around the corner
In the hallway
Always waiting
Waiting for something to go wrong

Death was always near
We got to know him intimately
More than you would ever want to
Someone you will never forget

In the hospital
Death visited parents
He took their babies

People I did not know
Crying from grief
I felt their pain
Because I knew
It could be me next time
My sweet baby gone

So many times
Praying constantly

Believing God would heal
God would save

So many miracles
So many times
Until that night
When Alicia was gone

My baby
I loved her so much
Gone to be with Jesus
Not here with us

Now I know grief
I am one of those parents

Death
I know him intimately
He has come to visit
Come to stay
Death is always with me
He is real
He took my baby
I loved her so much
More than you will ever know
But I couldn't love her enough
To keep her alive

Pictures
Memories
That's all I have

And Katie
I love her so much
She is my sweetie
One half of Katie and Alicia

Joe

44

Dealing with Anger

Anger.

It's the protective force that says, "Whoa, stand back, a boundary has just been violated."

It feels good, even if only momentarily.

It reminds you that you are still alive.

It's a way of releasing pent-up feelings.

It shows you care enough to express your outrage.

It's the truth in its uncut version, expressing honestly how you feel on the inside.

You have a right to be angry. Your baby died. You were cheated, "ripped off." You didn't get what you wanted. It's not fair. You don't like how your life partner only vaguely resembles her former self. You're pissed off. And you are acting it out

> by driving your car faster
>> by having little patience with whining coworkers
>> by not taking care of yourself.

Anger doesn't necessarily point a finger of blame at anyone in particular. It is very general, like kicking a dog when your wife is depressed and not wanting to communicate.

Even though anger is a normal emotion, that doesn't mean it's okay to act out your anger in ways that have negative effects on yourself or others. Too much anger (rage) or anger that smolders for too long without attention can cause harm to yourself and others. Don't deny that you are angry. But be aware of the potential to harm when anger is not managed appropriately, and learn how to let out some of the pressure.

Here are some tips from stress management experts on how to release stress caused by anger:

> *Walk it off.* Engage in some type of aerobic exercise (that you enjoy) like tennis, running, walking.

Eat it up. For instant stress reduction, eat soothing snacks that contain carbohydrates, sugars and starches, i.e., pretzels, jellybeans, crackers, popsicles. They contain an increased supply of serotinin, a brain chemical know for its calming effects. Avoid eating proteins. They thwart the production of serotinin.

Talk it through. Put words to your feelings. Find someone who won't tell you how they think you ought to feel or act, but will listen to your honest feelings.

Blow it out. Check your breathing. Are you holding your breath or taking shallow and quick breaths? Shallow breathing deprives your muscles of oxygen and causes tension. Breathe deeply, allowing oxygen to bathe and relax your muscles.

Melt it down. Tension causes muscles to tighten. Become aware of how your feels when it's tense, and then correct it on the spot. Learn how to relax. Shake your hands vigorously. You'll be amazed how quickly this can relieve tension. Treat yourself to a massage.

Cry it out. Tears come easily to some and not so easily to others. Try to see your tears as a gentle cleansing rain, washing away sorrow.

Let it go. You get to decide what to hold on to, why to hold on and how long you need to hold on. As long as you are holding on to something that isn't giving you positive energy, you don't have room for the things that could be life affirming to you.

Laugh it off. At some point you have to be able to see the humor in life itself. Life isn't just the front page of the paper; it's the comics, too. On the other side of tears, there is laughter, and vice versa.

*Never apologize for your feelings,
for to do so would be to
apologize for the truth.*

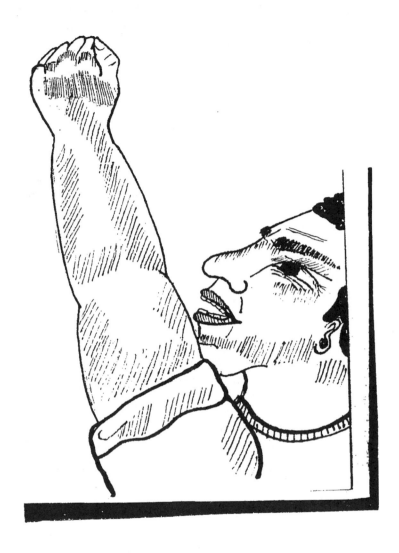

God, I'm taking the risk we seem only to take in secure and loving relationships; "I'm mad at you!"

I've somehow always made it through the crisis.
God gives me the strength to do what I need to
do for others,
but
afterward
when
everything is
taken care of,
the emptiness
breaks me
down.
Now, God
I ask
for
grace.

The Next Pregnancy

It may seem reasonable to go ahead and quickly initiate another pregnancy. Pregnancy may appear to be a quick way to fill that emptiness you are feeling, or to end the dreadful unhappiness, which threatens to consume your partner. However, most caregivers caution against rushing into pregnancy immediately after a loss. Grieving takes time, and adding anxieties of another pregnancy too soon is probably not wise.

Even after the worst part of the grieving is over, the two of you may still have difficulty agreeing how soon to start trying for another pregnancy, or whether you even want to get pregnant at all. Behind this ambivalence may be your fear of another loss and your reluctance to risk anything, which might disturb the emotional equilibrium the two of you have achieved, sending your partner off into another deep depression.

Sometimes, however, waiting is not in your best interest, because of advancing age or if you have a history of infertility. In this case, you are strongly advised to seek a subsequent pregnancy support group or individual counseling so you will have the extra help in place to carry you through a pregnancy that will be clouded by grief because of the previous loss.

Men tend to be outwardly optimistic about a subsequent pregnancy while women tend to talk about the pregnancy in more negative or tentative terms. Your partner's negative feelings may well have to do with protecting herself from getting burned again. At any rate, it can become annoying to hear her words of doom.

You will need to be strong enough to protect your partner from the misguided advice of those who will think your time of grieving should be over. And you will need to be tender toward your partner, listening attentively as she shares her fears.

49

I Don't Think of You as Often as I Should

I don't think of you as often as I should. I've built little reminders of you into my day. But I find myself reluctantly accepting that which I vowed would never happen: you are becoming a memory.

A year and a half later the sadness is still there, but it's sweeter. It's not all that much deeper beneath the surface, however. And while your new sister is not a replacement for you, my life is pretty much consumed with her right now – this one whom I hold just a little more closely, look in on one more time before I go to bed, and cherish in a special way I would never have imagined. In her face I find your own, especially when she sleeps.

Sometimes when you sister cries I think of you.
When her crying is getting on my nerves,
When I wish she would be quiet,
I remember how desperately I waited to hear you cry.
God, what I would have given for a sound to resonate
      in my memory of you.
So I hold her close,
Whisper "Daddy's right here,"
And think of you.

Jon Weaver

50

How Will This Loss Affect Your Work?

There will be no area in your life that will not be affected by your baby's death – including your work.

If you are fortunate you will get a few days off from work (bereavement leave). But unless you are able to make use of some extra leave time, you may find that, for financial reasons, you will have to go back to work before you feel ready. However, in general, fathers tend to need less recovery time than do mothers before returning to work.

When you go back to work, you can expect that you performance will be somewhat altered. Because you'll be thinking a lot about your baby who has died, you will probably have difficulty concentrating on your work. You will find yourself forgetting things and having little patience with pettiness in the work place. In addition, you may experience a lack of motivation or interest in your job.

You may not know what to say to people. Afraid of making others feel bad, you'll tend to refrain from saying anything at all, and then felt hat because you haven't spoken, you have betrayed the memory of your child.

You may be quite angry when people ask, "How's your wife?" without thinking to ask also about your well-being.

In your particular work situation, it may be that not everyone will have gotten the word that your baby died, so that even weeks or months later, someone will still ask, "How's the baby?" But as awkward as this query may by, you may feel even more resentful if a fellow worker doesn't say anything and you may wonder if he or she even knows, or remembers, or cares about your baby's death.

"How are you?"
Ask, and I'll hate you.
Don't ask, and I'll hate you.

If your co-workers are silent about your loss, it may be that they sincerely believe that they are helping you by not saying anything that they suppose would only add to your pain. Or they may be acting as may of us do around someone who has recently faced a tragedy. We feel awkward and uncertain what to do, so we just keep busy and pretend not to see the bereaved co-worker.

Work may also become an escape from the grief that awaits you at home. Some bereaved fathers tend to work more, rather than less, and find their employment to be healing or at least a helpful diversion.

After you have taken some time off from work so that you and your partner can be together and experience a real sense of closeness and interdependency, your partner may have feelings of abandonment and resentment when you go back to work. Especially if this shared tragedy has brought the two of you closer together than ever before, she may experience your absence as a further loss. Not only has she lost her baby, but now she is also going to lose the closeness that you so recently have begun to share. From her perspective, it may seem that because you are now free to go back to a normal life again, she's being left to do her grieving alone from now on.

Here are some suggestions:

Send announcement cards to your acquaintances so that they will all know about your loss at the same time. In some work situations, it may be possible to alert co-workers by memo or via the Internet.

If you can afford to, take your time before going back to work. Gradually work yourself back to a full schedule at your job.

Be willing to be the teacher, and let your co-workers know what you need from them.

Call your partner from work occasionally, just to check in.

When you come home form work, be mindful of your partner's mood. Ask her about her day and listen attentively.

How Long will Grief be Your Companion?

When will this nightmare of grief be over? How long will I have to suffer the pain of this grief? You aren't going to like the answer to these questions. The simple truth is that grief takes as long as it takes. Our experience is that for both mothers and fathers, grief lasts longer than they ever thought it would, and certainly longer than they want it to.

A clarification is in order here. For the most part, you don't ever get over grief; you get through it. And your objective in working through the grief is not to restore yourself to who you were before your baby died, but rather to readjust your life to the loss and to accommodate the new person that you will have become during this difficult experience.

And just as the manner of grief differs from person to person, so also does the duration of grief. Some persons get right into grief. They look at grief as a challenge to be met and a project to be completed. For such persons the intense grief usually doesn't last as long. Others play the game called, "If you can't see the hurt, then there isn't any." A wall goes up and emotions are shut away. Don't talk. Don't feel.

Intense grief is defined as a sense of hopelessness; mild grief is sadness. Most grieving parents have told us that their friends gave them permission to grieve for about a month. After that, the message was that they should be over feeling bad, and that it was time to get back to a normal life.

There will probably be a point at which time you'll have a similar feeling about your partner's grieving. You'll feel that this unhappiness has gone on long enough and you'll want her to be her old self again.

As a starting point, assume that your intense grief may take a few days to a couple weeks. Your partner's intense grief may last as long as two to three months. Your own grief will subside, but the family environment will depend on how long the grief affects you.

53

Her grief will most likely last a year, with intense periods of grief around anniversaries and holidays.

The first year after your baby's death will be filled with "first times" that never were, e.g. first Christmas, first birthday, first trip to the beach, first autumn, etc. Each one of these days is a potential occasion for renewed sadness, anger, resentment or anxiety. Even if you are personally not upset by the arrival of these occasions, your partner may well be affected, and you will become involved by default, whether you want to or not. Many people who have experienced grief say that the days leading up to a holiday are generally more difficult than the day itself. It will be helpful if you can keep these first days in mind and mention them to your partner before she mentions them to you.

You may decide that t would be good for the two of you to get away for a while, take a trip, enjoy a change of scenery, take a vacation from grief. Indeed, this may be just what you need. But before you make too many plans, take time to think about all the implications of such a venture. Leaving home may generate anxiety at a time when you most need the comfort of your own familiar surroundings. If you do go away, you may soon find yourselves wanting to turn around and come home.

Don't be surprised if you find yourself needing to take your baby's pictures or other precious memorabilia with you, because of your anxiety about being separated from them.

The most important thing to keep in mind as you travel this road of grief is that there are no guarantees, no set time schedules. And being strong doesn't mean not allowing yourself to experience emotions. Just because today is a good day, don't assume that tomorrow will be as satisfactory. Grief has many hills and valleys and the more you can just ride along, taking things as they come, the easier it will be for you. Trust that it will get better. Trust that you and your partner will learn and grow from this experience. And even after things get better and life looks sweeter, there will be times when your tender heart will remember the baby that too quickly passed through your life.

As a kid I learned that my brother and I could walk forever on a railroad track and never fall off – if we just reached across the track and held each other's hands.

Steve Potter

Looking Back

I was jealous of her because she was a woman. She got all the attention. I craved being validated for the huge loss in my life.

I wanted people to just know what I needed. I didn't want to have to tell them.

I feel like we have to "un-tell" people now.

Because I had been much more ambivalent about the pregnancy than she had been, I felt rather removed from the loss, while she was emotionally overwhelmed. I didn't know how to be with her. I wasn't prepared for the "un-bonding" experience that was about to happen.

This baby broke open my heart. I am forever grateful. Now I can experience joy at a deeper level than ever before.

I experienced a lot of guilt. I should have been more assertive with the hospital staff. I should have made them run more tests.

I wish I knew everything then that I know now. I've had to learn to forgive myself for not being the kind of dad I thought I would be.

I resented people telling me to take care of my partner.

I never had a physical connection with my dead baby, so I found myself groping after a spiritual connection.

My two greatest fears were first, that after suffering the loss of our baby, I would also lose my wife through divorce, and second, that I would forget this little person who had passed through our lives so quickly.

When no one else could keep her alive, I should have been able to.

I am trying to make something meaningful out of this.

I feel like it is a completed experience. I have not forgotten him, and what remains I will always take with me.

I was afraid we weren't going to make it. The times were pretty rocky.

She started relying more on other people, and I felt left out.

I had the mistaken idea that my own feelings weren't okay.

I wanted to take away her pain, but I couldn't. I wanted to feel how she felt. But I couldn't. I could take a break from it all and go downstairs and make myself a sandwich, but she couldn't.

It took me a long time to realize that my feelings were legitimate, too. I had no idea how she was feeling. She also had no idea how I was feeling.

When someone asked, "How's your wife?" part of me wanted to scream, "Hey, what about me? I feel pretty terrible, too!"

When someone asked how I was feeling, quite often I just said, "Okay." Did I say that because I wanted them to think I was really okay, even when I wasn't? Did I say it because I didn't want them to ask any more questions?

This experience has brought us closer together than we've ever been before, and it's taken us further apart than we've ever been before. I couldn't go to the place of grief where she was. I wasn't even sure I know who she was anymore.

The counselor asked my wife how I was doing because I seemed too upbeat considering what I was going through. I was doing the best I could with a terrible situation. The day our baby died, we had brought our four year old in with us so we could all find out together the gender of our baby. The news that something was wrong with the baby was a complete shock, and I had only done what seemed right. I had tried not to get emotional. I had tried to take care of our four year old. So I felt wrongly judged.

My dear wife,

I have so much to be grateful for since our daughter died. Early in our time of grief, somebody told us that someday we would see the gifts that our daughter brought to our lives. Those were empty words back then.

Now I understand...

My sadness doesn't frighten me as it once did.

And my anger doesn't disappoint me.

My weaknesses and mistakes don't leave me empty and discouraged.

Now I can tolerate rejection from others without always assuming it's a statement about me, and I'm learning to give others slack when they let me down.

Our lives are different. I can't deny that. I want to honor that because in doing so, I honor our precious gift giver.

Your loving husband

Another Pieta

*Tender as
the new growth
that springs forth,
he bends and
embraces life
and all that
it has to
teach him.*

Internet Resources

Please Note:
The following website listings are current as of January, 2020.
Listings frequently change so if you find one of these sites
unavailable, please do a search for the information you are seeking
using a search engine like Google or Bing.

The M.I.S.S. Foundation is a nonprofit, volunteer based organization committed to providing emergency support to families in crisis after the death of their baby or young child from any cause. www.missfoundation.org

Griefnet has over 50 email support groups to help to people work through loss and grief issues of many kinds. www.griefnet.org

Multiple Births offers bereavement support for parents who have lost one, more or all of their multiple birth children during pregnancy. https://jumelle.ca/resources-for-families-expecting-twins-multiples/bereavement-support-2/

Share: Pregnancy and Infant Loss Support Inc. The mission of SHARE is to serve those whose lives are touched by the tragic death of a baby through miscarriage, stillbirth or newborn death. www.nationalshare.org

Perinatal Loss/Grief Watch (that's us) offers resources for parents experiencing a pregnancy loss, or for anyone who is grieving. www.griefwatch.com

Additional Resources from Grief Watch

Heart Prints

These handmade ceramic hearts were first introduced with the option of a handprint or footprint (in blue or pink), but have now been broadened to include angel, butterfly, dragonfly, cross or paw print (only available in white). They are a nice way to say "I remember."

The Remembering Heart

Two beautiful handcrafted ceramic hearts in one. When separated, the tiny inner heart can be placed with the loved one who has died as a reminder of their unbroken connection to those who remain behind. They can also be tied together to form a necklace of love around the loved one. The outer heart is kept by the bereaved and can be worn on a necklace, acknowledging their grief.

Hole in My Heart

A simple brightly colored ceramic heart with a hole in it. Made for those who want to show that they are not "complete" and that someone very special is missing in their life.

Certificate of Life

Delicately embossed, with iridescent stars, flowers and a weeping teddy bear, these cream colored certificates acknowledge both the death and life of your baby. Available style options are Miscarriage, Stillborn and Neonatal Loss. A way to remember this baby was real, was wanted, was loved.

Singing Ornaments

Imagine your loved one cradled in a star or by an angel. Our textured white ceramic ornaments make noise whenever they move. They can be used as a holiday ornament, a wind-chime, or as a remembering gift to loved ones. Available ornaments include Angel, Heart, Star, Butterfly, Dragonfly, Bell or Tree. You can also personalize you Singing Ornament by adding a birthstone to the heart or star at its center.

We Were Gonna Have a Baby, But We Had an Angel Instead.

A children's book told from a young child's perspective about the excitement and dreams of a coming baby, and the disappointment and sadness of a miscarriage. Beautiful ink and watercolor illustrations.

Someone Came Before You

A book for the child who comes after a sibling who died. It's a perfect gift just for them. It explains in a gentle way the parents' desire for a child and the sadness that comes over them when that baby dies. Includes suggestions about keeping your baby's memory alive.

Tear Soup, a recipe for healing after a loss

One of the most unique aspects of Tear Soup is that it speaks to every generation while demonstrating the universality of grief. If you are new to grief, Tear Soup will help you to understand the issues that grief presents. If you are bereaved, you will feel understood. The "tips" section in the back of the book is rich with wisdom and concrete recommendations. 56 pages of beautiful, heartfelt illustrations.

Strong and Tender

A book especially for fathers, this is a collection of insights, helpful hints and tender thoughts to give a father strength during the dark times of grief following his baby's death. For too long fathers have been the forgotten grievers. By giving him this special book you tell him you also recognize his loss.

Still to be Born

Addresses the needs of the couple who are still longing for a baby, but afraid of being hurt again by another loss. Among the many topics covered in this 120-page book are: Why mourn the loss of someone you never knew? How soon should you attempt another pregnancy? What kind of feelings do most women have during another pregnancy? What are the chances of the same thing happening again?

A Grandparent's Sorrow

Grandparents suffer a double loss. Your child is grieving and so are you. Included in this booklet are suggestions on how grandparents can help themselves as they grieve, how to better understand their child during this difficult time, and how to hold close the precious memory of their grandchild.

Personalized Birth Announcements

When words don't come easily....

The birth of your child is important, even if your child died too soon. You may still want to send a birth announcement that lets people know of your child's brief life. These 3.5"x5" cards are a special way to help your friends and relatives know about and share your sorrow. We will make every effort to complete your order and mail it by priority mail within 24 hours after we receive it.

You give us all the information that you want included in your message and we do the rest. Your return address is printed on the envelopes at no extra charge. Please tell us how you want your names to appear on the envelope. (Minimum order 2 packages @ $15.00 for a package of 10.)

In an attempt to cover the wide array of feelings that you may be experiencing, we provide a variety of text options for both the front and inside of your Personalized Announcements. We hope that you find one that helps you to share your story with others. However, if you do not find text that fits your situation, or if you just prefer to share your story in your own words, we also offer the option to create your entire card in your own words.

Please visit our website for more information and to place your order: www.griefwatch.com.